Acknowledgements are due to the editors of the following:

Answering Back (Picador), *London Magazine*, *London Review of Books*, *Manchester Review*, *New Welsh Review*, *nth Position*, *Paging Dr Jazz* (Shoestring Press), *Poetry London*, *Poetry Review*, *Poetry Wales*, *Speaking English, poems for John Lucas* (Five Leaves Press), *The Times Literary Supplement*, *Warwick Review*.

Some of these poems have been read on BBC Radio 4.

CAFÉ DES ARTISTES

POETRY
Hidden Identities
Bright River Yonder
Cornerless People
Double
Ignoble Sentiments
Canada
Spending Time With Walter
Blues
The Ship

PROSE POEMS
Mystery in Spiderville

TRANSLATION
Censored Poems by Marin Sorescu
(with Hilde Ottschofski)

AS EDITOR
Teach Yourself Writing Poetry
(with Matthew Sweeney)

CAFÉ DES ARTISTES

John Hartley Williams

CAPE POETRY

Published by Jonathan Cape 2009

2 4 6 8 10 9 7 5 3 1

Copyright © John Hartley Williams 2009

John Hartley Williams has asserted his right under the Copyright, Designs
and Patents Act 1988 to be identified as the author of this work

First published in Great Britain in 2009 by
Jonathan Cape
Random House, 20 Vauxhall Bridge Road,
London SW1V 2SA

www.rbooks.co.uk

Addresses for companies within The Random House Group Limited can be found
at: www.randomhouse.co.uk/offices.htm

The Random House Group Limited Reg. No. 954009

A CIP catalogue record for this book is available from the British Library

ISBN 9780224087858

The Random House Group Limited supports The Forest Stewardship
Council (FSC), the leading international forest certification organisation.
All our titles that are printed on Greenpeace approved FSC certified paper
carry the FSC logo. Our paper procurement policy can be found at:
www.rbooks.co.uk/environment

Mixed Sources
Product group from well-managed
forests and other controlled sources
www.fsc.org Cert no. TT-COC-2139
© 1996 Forest Stewardship Council

Typeset in Bembo by Palimpsest Book Production Limited,
Grangemouth, Stirlingshire

Printed and bound in Great Britain by
MPG Books Ltd, Bodmin, Cornwall

Pour yourself a glass of vino
Beech trees fall and squirrels go
And men in hats collect the debris
And on the stump there sits a crow

CONTENTS

CAFÉ DES ARTISTES

BACCHUS

My old friend! Your gut protuberant,
                             your horns
palely curved, your tongue claret-sticky –
how good it is to see you! Take
                        the weight off your rump.
I think we've listened to this plopping
                           music before,
have we not? This lucid glugging?
Tall-stemmed glasses catching fire from light?

So who'll drink first? You or me?
How specific our thirst is – for just this raisin,
just this weedy fragrance, the tanninic
                        beatitudes of wine!
Do we abjure the proletariat of corn and hops?
                           We do!
Wine is how words taste, fermented in darkness,
releasing tongues from cobwebs that restrained them.

Old friend, I can see by the look on your face
                             you've
something to tell me. Good or bad? Speak!

CAFÉ DES ARTISTES

Mr Loneliness takes his usual seat
at the corner furthest from the door,
and moves the pepper pots aside
for a better view of the floor.

Waiting is what you do there
for a waiter who'll never come,
for a dish they've not invented yet,
for everyone, or anyone.

Waiting is what you do there
– attentively, or somnolently, with your fly
undone, or different coloured socks,
or a mustard-spattered tie.

The proprietor will soon emerge
to play his shrunken concertina
on which he captures seabird noises, or
the hoots of sinking steamers.

He'll accompany his honkings
with lyrics full of death and sex.
Fowl and flesh fly fast, or scamper nimblier
down the throats of guests.

And then he'll lift his matelot skirts
and do a hornpipe side by side
with Mr Loneliness, who feels again
the Angel of his Muse alive.

Using pepper pots as castanets,
spotless napkin tucked into his pocket,
Mr Loneliness dances as the ceiling fan
goes slowly round: *ockit ma-lockit ma-lockit . . .*

Who is this melancholy fellow?
This exo-skeleton? This rickety artiste
of tentacles and ink? They gawp, the customers,
to see such spectral leapings at the feast –

a hatstand sort of fellow, where the hats
of long-gone customers are tossed,
the scarves of women and the coats of bankers,
all the lost apparel of the lost . . .

Till silence follows music, except
the widdershins-revolving fan that ticks
its copper-bladed swastika and makes
a noise that someone really ought to fix.

THE DRUNKEN BOAT

after Arthur Rimbaud

Down the blank indifference of the rivers
I suddenly lost weigh, my hauliers had vanished –
Naked, nailed to gaudy totem poles, they'd been
Used by screeching redskins for a target.

As for the sailors – ferrymen of Flemish
Corn or English wool – I didn't give a damn.
When their racket and the hauliers had gone
The rivers let me sail where I pleased.

Me, last winter, deafer than children's brains,
Into the frenzied lashings of the tides
I ran! Never were cast-adrift peninsulas
Subjected to a chaos more triumphant!

The storm blessed my ocean-going rebirths.
Lighter than a cork, I danced the waves –
Those rollers of corpses, eternal. Ten nights
And never a pang for an imbecile lighthouse eye!

Sweeter than sour apple-flesh to children,
The green water breached my pinewood hull;
Splashes of blue wine, bolts of vomit cleansed me,
Swept away my rudder and my anchor.

Since then, I've bathed in the Poem of the Sea,
Infused with stars, milky, devouring the green azures
Where sometimes pale and ravished remnants
Of a drowned man meditatively churn and sink;

Where brief-tinctured bluenesses and madness thrive;
Where slow rhythms underneath the dazzling day –
Stronger than alcohol, more great than song –
Ferment the bitter rednesses of love!

Skies fissured by lightning, I've known,
And spouts, and tide-cracks and currents,
And dawns released like flocks of doves.
Sometimes I saw what men believed they saw!

I've seen the low sun, stained with mystical horrors,
Freeze in its violet spotlight's far-flung beam
– Like actors posturing in ancient dramas –
The venetian-blinded shimmering of waves!

I've dreamed the green night of dazzled snows,
Slow-rising kisses reaching the eyes of seas,
The upswelling gush of unheard-of sap,
The blue and yellow flares of singing phosphorus!

Months I followed the mad mooings
Of the reef-battering swell. I never thought to question
How radiant feet of virgin Marys were treading down
The brutish snouts of asthma-gasping Oceans!

Listen, I struck incredible Floridas, where
The eyes of man-skinned panthers melted into flowers!
Where reins longer than rainbows drove
Bug-eyed cattle under the horizon of the seas!

I saw boilings of immeasurable swamps, nets
Where whole Krakens putrefied in bending grasses!
I saw erupting waters implode the calms
And distances fall cataracting into depths!

Glaciers, silver suns, pearling waves, charcoal-glowing skies!
Awesome beachings on the floor of brown gulfs,
Stinking termites devouring giant sea-snakes
Falling from twisted trees, perfumed black!

If only I'd shown to children those sea-bream
Of the blue wave, those golden fish, those singing fish.
– The spindrift of flowers cradled my drifting;
Mysterious breezes gave me momentary wings.

A martyr, sometimes, wearied of poles and zones,
My rolling sweetened by sobs of the sea, I felt its
Shadow-flowers press their yellow cupping glass
Against me, and I lulled there, like a woman kneeling . . .

An island, almost, the squabbles and droppings
Of screaming blonde-eyed birds bouncing off my planks.
I roved, and through my frail ropes
The drowned descended backwards into sleep! . . .

Me, thus, shipwrecked in an inlet's tangled hair,
Hurricane-hurled at the birdless air,
Me, that neither lifeboat nor passing ship could save,
A carcase, drunk on water;

Free, stinking, clambering from violet mist,
Me, drilling a hole in the reddened wall of skies,
Smothered in sun-fungus, livid streams of snot –
The exquisite jam of brilliant poets! –

Me, running, stained with the lunar electric,
Mad sailboard, with a black sea-horse escort,
When July-cudgelled skies were beaten down,
Ultramarine into fiery funnels;

Me, trembling, feeling the howling rut
Of beasts and whirlpools fifty leagues off,
Eternal weaver of blue standstills,
Longing for Europe, its ancient parapets!

Archipelagoes of stars, islands of raving skies,
I've seen you open to those who wander:
– Is it in these bottomless nights you sleep, exile yourself,
Million birds of gold, O strength of the future? –

I've wept too much! Dawns are a heartbreak,
All moonlight an atrocity, the sun is bitter;
I'm drunk with languor, swelled from the prick of love.
Let my keel split! Let me founder in the deep!

If I desire one water of Europe, it is the black
Cold puddle where, in scented dusk,
A squatting child full of sadness, launches
A boat as frail as a butterfly in May.

No longer, waves, can I bathe in your moods,
No longer plough the cotton-freighter's wake,
No longer sail beneath the hubris of a flag,
Nor skiff below the dread-eyed prison-ships.

OSTRICH PALISADES

There they are: the feathered neck-poles driven
solid into ground. You can't expect a man to linger
in the shadow of their beaky crenellations long.
Beneath their bending ramparts
dice-cups move from hand to hand. The horses blether:
defend, defend, defend. Defend.

In darkness someone slits a dress from knee to breast.
Better don't protest. The pewter adjutants,
slate-grey corporals – brimstone's acolytes –
bunch up to slake their thirst for fire and cards
and gamble maidenhoods against the desert sand
that leaps and drifts against the walls of cartilage.

One would like to leave. Strip off his epaulettes,
tear the raging buttons from his jacket, expel
the roebuck panegyric from his head, refute the litany
of drinking songs, apply a poultice to the stable-cries
that sear his listening ears through straw.
Get out of there.

That lump. That built-up shadow, amassing out of
shadow-earth. That castle baulked against a universe of nothing.
Don't think that as he walks, discarding boots, un-
buckling sword, he wilfully abjures
the whole refractory. He accepts the night's uprooted flowers,
their shapes dashed hard against his mind,

and petals make ideas of blossom bloom: the Rose of
Betelgeuse, Orion Buttercup, their fragile being
rolled in by the rut of beasts. His bootless tread
leads out beyond the ostrich gate, a whisper-progress

into emptiness where stars hang colour
no one but the star-entranced can see.

You can't expect a man simply to win or die.
Insignias torn off, he mooches barefoot
over rabbit bones and scorpions and cooling rock,
and breathes the thistly air without regret.
Behind him, vast against the moon, smelling of arrest,
they rise up to a dungeon sky: the ostrich palisades.

NEAR DOVE COTTAGE

You won't believe this. I'm living
in the hovel two doors up
from William Wordsworth's old place,
and this morning through a whisky
headache I heard a polar bear sniffing
the mint round the front door and gruffing
a sort of chortle-cum-puff with a
touch of growl, so I let it in.
It shouldered past me and swung
up the stairs to the bathroom,
stuck its head in the toilet, then into
the bath, ate a notebook of new poems,
slithered downstairs and sprawled
onto the length of cheap Ikea fabric
I've covered the horrible sofa with.

Listen bear, I said. How you got here,
and where you came from, is your
business, but you have to go.
I stared into its black eyes and couldn't
decide if it was intelligence or nothing
that came reflected back – or something
I maybe didn't want to know about.
I could smell the whale lagoon drift
of its breath. Then it whacked
my table with a loosely-swinging paw
and a plate of half-eaten sausages
hit the carpet. It yawned and I observed
its violet tongue. Listen Son-of-Wordsworth
it said, and I realised it was imitating me,
don't you realise the ice is melting?
My brothers are all adrift on loose pack ice
and when that starts to melt . . .

It looked at the sausages on the floor.
I've dined, it said, off John Keats,
I made a light meal of Samuel Taylor Coleridge.
Couldn't catch Shelley – he was too quick,
the Wordsworths were simply indigestible,
and the last thing polar bears need
(I could see it was choosing its words)
is all that sweet-toothed stuff about love and nature.
We need realism deeper than the planet's core,
the kind you can't even dig for
till you've thrown away your spades.

I gazed at the bear. It couldn't stay.
I had visitors coming. What would they think?
Then it devoured a chair. Two great
chomps of its bull-muzzle, the thing was gone.
It also ate my table, books and only cactus.
Then it commenced to eat the stairs.
Look, I said, while the cottage
was munched around me. I'm supposed
to be writing poems here, how can
I do that if you eat the furniture?
It growled terribly then, and demolished
walls, floors, chimney-stacks,
and we stood in the cool light, on bare terrain,
and it reared up on its back paws,
and the fathomless rupture of a great noise
tremored through the beef of its body,
a roar like icebergs calving, or a world
simply breaking asunder, and I stared up
blankly into something else.

POETS

sit
on doorsteps,
not thinking
about the next line of a poem.

They go
to the seaside
just like other people.
You have to admire the way
they walk into the sea
when the red flag is up.

The surf is heavier
than Milton's
blank verse,
and the poets are out there
riding it.
If I were a lifeguard
I would certainly blow my whistle.
But there they are, the poets,
taming those foam horses
as if they were
breaking in
the metres of God.

★

Or something.

★

Later they walk
past shop windows.
Poets, the Italian suits
and the French wines
in this elegant resort
are almost certainly
worth more than your lives.
It's hardly a wonder
your language is down to a whisper.
There's so much
wry meekness
in your encroachments
on the silence:

'I have everything
I need
for my
requirements,
thank you.'

What a statement!
What brevity!
What profundity!
No wonder people
simply can't hear you!

*

Poets don't say
what they mean.
They don't mean what they mean.
They don't say what they say.
They don't even mean
what they say they mean.
They don't even say

what they seem to be meaning to say.
Meaning is saying.
Saying is meaning.
Something like that, anyway.

This is unfortunate.
People are baffled.
Poets, how dearly
you would like to leap
like circus tigers
through the hoop of people's bafflement
and alight agilely
on the other side!

★

Have you addressed a poet recently?
I think not.
In fact, no one has spoken to the poet.
No one has seen the poet lately.
No one has read the last book.
Or if they have read it, they were puzzled by it.
It is good to be creative,
but what is it all about?
People play bridge, these days.
Or they drive their cars at defenceless pedestrians.
Or they go to the cinema.
Does one really need
to try and understand the poet
when the poet claims
no effort is needed, when the poet
maintains, in fact, that effortlessness
is the soul
of what the poet does?

★

One fears one is being hoodwinked.

★

In the cemetery
it is very cold.
There's an icy wind
powdering the graves
with snow.
Who do these footsteps belong to?
What is this mumbling?
Whose shadow is sneaking
spectrally through trees?
No, no! Absolutely wrong!
It's not a poet! It's a mourner!
The poet is safely at home,
sitting in front of a fire,
drinking a little mulled wine,
reading an excellent poem
by a dead rival.
Very soon
there's a little tapping at the window.
Tap-tap, tap-tap, tap-tap.
A slow smile walks across the face of the poet.
Who could that be?
What could that knocking signify?

The poet turns
the handle

and opens the door . . .

PORT

The poets are leaving,
wheeling their strange bags
to the harbour's edge.

A man in a vest
is leaning from a window,
throwing crumbs to pigeons.

Everywhere
it stinks
of fish.

Dragging their ankles
through shadows of the Custom House,
the poets are leaving.

At the quay's end,
they stand
scanning the sky for a sail.

Over café tables,
a descending canopy
scythes back sunlight.

In colourless rooms,
the widows lock up
decanters of the dark red wine.

HIS LIFE IN STRING

for Matthew Sweeney

What did they knit,
those women round the guillotine?

A man of double-purls
of lazy-daisies, cable-stitch, French knots
a man of holes made plain
in click-reticulated cashmere
a webbed man stuffed with gunny and nankeen
a fiery Fawkes in craquelure
a pleached man, darned and meshed and interwisted
a crew-necked fellow, twine
unravelling in spit and brine,
aristocratic weirdo member of the tell-the-truth club
(cackles of the *sans-culottes* ringing in his severed brain)
a Welsh-knitted man
spurting warm hereditary druid-blood, the thread of red
unspooling as the bobbin jerks,
the blade's implacable descending thump
– 'a little light refreshment at the neck' –
a bowling ball released along the alley of the mind
toward the glow of ever-fading meaning,
skittle-fingers of those crones
crouching there to crochet him: decapitated sweater-man
mumbling anti-technologically-minded poems
muttering the rip and rib of life
arms flung out
empty of the flesh that filled them –
this discarded, headless jumper-man of poetry
tossed indifferently here
upon the back of your old wicker chair.

DON'T TOUCH ANYTHING

The man who changes a landscape
by moving a stone, has changed it.
The house is built of stone on stone.
Hungrily, ivy seizes the wall.

The bell sounds for an assembly.
Someone has come to change the world.
The view to a plain, from a high window,
reveals the dust of a coming army.

Cries happen. The sky is troubled.
The broken fragments of a house
jostle, now, with weeds and saplings.
From a cracked floorplan, a village grows.

A gust of renewal. The breeze
through stirring grass emits
a fiercer exhalation than the words
which promise promises.

Except for the downward propulsion
that is in them, the words have no meaning.
Their gravity is hidden from their users.
No one is content to stay where he is.

The city swallows the village
and is, in turn, destroyed. Birds cruise
the Autumn plain and fall
to the severe mouth of thunder.

A lizard blinks from a window crack.
Cobwebs drowse in the sunlight.
Between sleep and attention, the lizard's
rapid throat breathes silence.

There is a feeling no one has spoken,
as if arrested by supreme shyness,
an intimation someone would like to speak,
wind through stubble, a legendary sigh . . .

Behind the blank opening of a door
made dark by sunshine, the proprietor
is standing in a pool of shadow
like one who must be impelled into the light.

Existing always on the edge of extinction,
it will be important to remember the next step
so the fall of a leaf may still be heard
by someone who should not be in the orchard.

INSTRUCTIONS FOR REACHING
THE SEA

Pass through the olive groves
but keep your dog on the leash.
Climb to the chapel on Cypress Hill –
that's a *via Dolorosa* you've just climbed.
Vipers, at least, are visible here,
not so with the tick.
Should one fall invisibly from leaves,
deposit eggs beneath your skin,
your walk will stroll you into meningitis.
Don't think about this.
You can't see the sea for the pines.
Endure their creaking.
Your thermos is empty. Your sandwiches chewed.
Some sheep scared upwards
have utterly vanished. Descend,
my friend, and cross that stream.
You're into trespass now.
The gamekeeper will claim
he thought you were a stag.
That castle that confronts you –
its dusky turrets swarm with bats.
Don't jam their equipment,
by phoning for help
or you will die, vampirically, in night-bites.
Get over those gates
to the highway beyond.
Appreciate the moon, its huge
unsmiling orb. Enter the town
with its padlocked shops.
Ah, there's a sunset fading to fire
across the bay, where a factory chimney
is sending a pillar of smoke straight up.

A lifeguard, morose, has a dog
that is growling at yours,
and waves play a tune on the shingle.
No need to break into a run.
Put the dog, with its forward-pointing nose,
in the prow of a rowboat, and steal it.
Now skiff for all your worth.
Under your seat
there's an oilskin package.
Open it.
Read by a wobble of moonlight:
INSTRUCTIONS FOR REACHING THE LAND

THE READER

The reader finds himself in an old Europe,
in a shadowy night of lamps and chairs
through which long-aproned waiters glide.
He's drifting on a poem of resistance,
on a curved elegance of crooked symmetries,
on a game of words that meets head on
both gag and bullet, and does not flinch.

But revellers make him restless. They
untether him, who is not tied. Smash-
mechanical, a factory music builds up walls
against the silent dream the pages hold
where words spring fresh into the tumult,
a noiseless fall of water, drowning sound.
The reader sits, and makes his tipple last.

Down empty boulevards at night,
crossing windy squares with tall *Laternen*,
his thoughts meet strollers like himself, who nod.
He occupies the lamp-throw of a language
that lights a hubbub and a wineglass,
a barely occupiable chair. He lets
the pages of his book fall very slowly shut.

The poet's face upon the cover
looks back in quizzical avoidance.
His lips describe a shadow in the light.
The reader stands and puts the volume
in his pocket. He pushes out toward the exit,
past all the young, the drunk, the happy
who fill the night with selves that do not read.

London 22. vi. 07

THE GARDEN OF IAN
HAMILTON FINLAY

Beautiful terrorist
Apollo's golden head in the leaves
Aircraft-carrier birdtable
           armed to the crumb
Swastika pool of the mind

The hills are distant as arctic dogs
A whiplash of wind crosses their brow
Feel the birch of the breeze
The season is late, flowerless,
                luxuriant

A last look
Remembers an image of richness
Martial fecundity, a stern profusion
                 where
Epigraphs are naturally stone

MIDSUMMER NIGHT

Well,

that was
a massive birdstrike on my car –
pigeon-shit everywhere,
or was it seagulls?

I got in
and peered out
through vertical guano streaks –
a prisoner behind white bars.

At the carwash,
I dropped in the hard ticket,
flinched at the foam-attack
as it seethed across the windscreen.

Woolly rotundas
beat upon my door.
Had I lowered the aerial?
Were the windows shut?

Afterwards
in the evening light
I inspected the age-crazed paintwork.
Had I washed off my luck?

Two boys appeared
with voices enclosed in cardboard
and begged a lift
to a party they were late for.

We sailed over Wandsworth
booming with laughter –
an equine troop
on its way to a masque.

And people stopped
to point at nodding donkey-heads
rollicking gravely by
in the back of my Ford Titania.

REQUIEM FOR A PRINCESS

(i)

A penguin, a donkey, a piano.
Their tinkle-plonky grief.

A station trolley
rumbling over pavement slabs
carries the deceased.

Black hearse, black iceberg
in a warm dissolving ocean,
it sails toward the gulf
that it will occupy.

The flag is folded small,
the folding of a child. Smoothed
from the national laundry
is a crease.

The penguin. Its raised beak.
Its self-important air. An advice bird.

Rising trumpets lift up
through shafts of attic sunlight.
Sound-motes. The air is soothed.
Chords on dusty keys.

There she goes!
Straight as a die!

Tantara!

(ii)

A press of the old
against the young, craning
necks to watch
the sombre rigadoon.

More friends she had
than secret yellows on a wasp,
ghosting
the popular tune.

The shouts of a Sergeant-Major
wheel the regiment.
What are the thoughts of a serving man?
Tender? Insolent?

Their black trousers
are striped with gold.

(iii)

Here is the man in the stovepipe hat
who is writing this poem.

Surreptitiously,
a pouch of verses round his neck,
he has joined the procession
astride a donkey.

Downward

into the bone
of her creaturely self

he is melting,
against his will . . .

(iv)

Ever see, the penguin remarks, *so many poems, candles . . . ?*
The donkey twitches its ear.
Don't happen to play the piano, by any chance? the penguin asks.
The donkey twitches its ear.

A little hoof-clatter
on the ivories?
A jig? A reel? A little bonzo
up-and-at-'em stomp?

Donkey fixes penguin
with long, donkey regard.

We need a melody
sweet as it is clumsy.
We need a song
that does it with its thumb . . .

Donkey moves to piano stool,
lifts the lid with teeth.

Yeah! cries the penguin.
Hoof it, Jack!

(v)

Big feet on the keys.
Ragtime, hot and strong.

Or axes to the splinters
of a sounding board.

At rigid attention,
the penguin stands,

mouthing the words
of a piano-smashing song.

Synch your lips
to text without reprise.

(vi)

On a 94 bus, a donkey.
Wossat? asks a passenger.
Never seen no donkey before? the conductor asks.
Not on a bus, says the passenger.
Well you have now, says the conductor.
He checks the traveller's season,
who alights, subsequently, at the junction
of Goldhawk Road and King Street.
That a piano I hear? asks the passenger.
Not on my bus, the conductor yells.

Everyone inside
wishes they would stop.

(vii)

Alice wilds the pack.
The donkey does not move.

Court cards blown
across a wiry back

snow it out of grey.
Where the donkey stands,

argent on a field, fesse,
heraldry becomes the land,

a colourful finesse
of King, Queen, Jack

or floral coat of arms
ushering the fade to black.

Wolves look up from their bones.
Flowers ruffle to a night-breeze.

A lunar ray
striking the face of an owl

catches in its waspy gaze
reflections of the slow disband

of mourners clutching discards,
. . . hers . . . his . . . these . . .

September 1997

WHITE ASPARAGUS

Waking in the empty house,
he was convinced that she had knocked.
But no one stood behind the opened door.
The trees were new with green.

Rubbing his eyes, he decided it was
spring. The Polish workers, slouched down
in the big yellow double-deckers,
had arrived from Gdansk to cut the crop.

He walked out to the edge of the field.
Underground, the spears were being lifted
by practised hands. The severed phalluses
jolted by in the back of a tractor.

No sunlight, no chlorophyll. The barrows
reminded him of burial grounds.
The stooping toilers worked with
money's concentration in their knives.

If only he could be certain that from
time to time she thought of him. A cyclist
pedalled the horizon. He glimpsed
the flashing coruscations of its wheel.

But if she was dead? It had been a long time.
He wondered how the vegetable had tamed mankind.
How it had seduced men and women.
How it had invented butter.

Beelitzer Spargel. He thought of himself,
burrowing in the dark, his body untouched by light,
perfectly pale. And of the harvester's skilled
hand, sliding down to his root.

RADIO FUN

Warm cabinet of sound
be known again to me.
Let *Cushion Foot Stomp* forever haunt
the stag-faced lobby
of Godalming Hotel.
O radio tune thyself
to voices Britisher than mine –
clarity-bones and banana-tones
not to mention zeal.
Talk me through the mystery.
Give me Music While I Snooze.
Let me hear the spaceman's words
go wonky as the dullness
of a sermon from St Ethelreda's
monsters him completely.
Let John Arlott
tamper with the seam
and deal out chaos to the pitch
as umpires shrug
and raise a finger at the moon.
Have Billie sing the blues,
my father grab the off switch,
while I defend till death
her melancholy-jocund squawk.
I want the weather to be dismal.
Let half of Cornwall disappear,
and London, under fog so thick,
you hardly hear
that Hilversum
is reaching out in Dutch to rescue us.
Hilversum. O Hilversum.

Bright prairie of foreign names,
let me ride your range.
Let your voices draw closer
to the chair of my ear
where I crouch
in white attention.
Let me rise through listening,
a phoenix out of boredom's ashes,
to hear *The Washboard Five*
shoot antlers off
The Monarch of the Glen.
Have everybody
duck.
Wireless, be my guarantee
there'll be
something I can like round here.
Let that waitress slide
with me together
down the moaning curves
of Buster Bailey's clarinet
to roam the illustrated dial, the world
that whispers far away.
O let me press
the baffle of your speaker fabric
to my far gone ear. Have
ocean breakers
and a mew of seagulls waft
me to a tryst upon a raft
with someone else who likes
a toady tune
like me . . .

JAZZ RECIPE

Bring your father back to life. Strut
the kitchen, prodigal and wild. Bash
with wooden spoons a taradiddle
on your pans and Kilner jars. Conjure up
the jazz that drove him furious, then tip
a glass of calming trouble in the mix.
Drop confetti made from crosswords in.
Waste what's valuable. And stir!

Tufts from an old mortar-board, you'll need,
and vague reproaches from the lady
who composed his wife. You'll also need
the mystic phrases he'd incant into the air
whenever things went badlier than bad –
Drans, drans, ay theng yow verrry kindly!
Bubbling hard? Then hurl eleven raisins in the pot
and chant eleven names – the Wolves of long ago.

Now drizzle in a secret female voice –
her husky memories of the horse's role
in literature (and over jumps, and down the straight).
Strew into the brew a tipster's view of womanhood.
Is a bilious foam galloping round copper sides?
Can you feel the savour of those pippings at the post?
Invoke the Imp of Babel, his furrowed sister Groan.
Perform the Rite of Bollocks with a ladle.

Time to goad your daddy with your ignorance.
A howl of yelp will gurgle from the pot.
A twisting shadow-column will rise and spin
across the ceiling. Your magic's worked!
It's a face you know, puzzled and concerned,

pale fingers pulling on a gingery moustache,
wrinkled with distaste for oompah and excess.
Morris Oxford, it says. Austin Devon.

Throttle the gas. Arrest those ladle-loopings.
Can't have that look of *I told you so*
floating there like Mrs Beeton's conscience.
Douse the sniffs. Cap the sighs. Reduce the pan
to silent grumps of cool. No answers to
questions now. Slabber trickles down pantry walls.
Good cooks know authenticity. They know. So
draw a chair up to the kitchen table. Grieve.

BONEHENGE

Millicent Bean and her lover, Pete
(of *Pete's Klutches-While-U-Wayte*)
disturb the long grass round a neolith
at midnight, under a lupine moon.

Millicent wants to savour ghosts
of ancient rites. She'd like to meet
the Blind Rat of Vision,
the Nibbling Fieldmouse of Doom.

Pete has other things upon his mind.
Under slabs that lean above them,
narrowing to clasp a lunar view,
they lie together on a weedy stone.

Horizontal, pale, cupidinously
wrought, they fire their love-cries
in puny prayers upwards through
a moon-addressing megaphone.

Stretched and gasping, pleasured
images of nihilous fertility, they lie.
The pewter orb is pinched and held
as if by jeweller's fingers: a pearl.

From the disappointed caves of everything, resurrected ritualists arise
and reach out bony claws to grasp
Pete's ankles, Millicent's quicksilver curls.

Over astral surfaces, snakes of iodine
and cobalt flow. Fatly shimmering desire

trembles for a shape it cannot reach.
A cry, and humans start to grieve.

The pincer stones release the moon.
It floats on by to other trysts.
Coition's after-sadness stains the ground
with shadows that repel the weave

of tangled limbs that shrink away like
snailhorns touched, or shrivelling worms,
into their labyrinth. You OK? asks Pete.
Millicent pulls grass and twigs from hair.

LAST LETTER TO ZOU-ZOU

Zou-Zou, you were the eyes of my otherness,
                              my altitude's parole,
the spine of my prickly sabotage,
                      the nip in my airy taboo.
Your naked legs across my shoulders
                      made a burden of questions
and the answers loved to hide
              so we chased them into view.

But now it's quieter than leaf-fall
            and the wind has mysteriously dropped
and I'm driving alone
        up the empty street of Shattersley-le-Hope
toward a heavy Yorkshire sky
                  where a traction engine's flywheel
tugs a harrow over ploughland
                      and all I can see is the slope

taking me into the railway hills
                  fast enough to make sure
no cool telegraphist will catch me
                  smoking along the ridge,
disturbing a flock of crows
            that fracture the landscape to blacks
like jigsaw pieces of cloudburst
              or cracks in a deep-sworn pledge.

This is me, Zou-Zou, swerving the curves
                  of my entire alphabet for you,
addressing you with a squeal of wheels,
              cheeks hollowed out by the gravity of speed,

goggles agleam with *St Molten's Fire*,
                              going faster than I'd like to go slow,
a man getting closer and closer
                    to a finishing line that recedes.

I'm racing a storm, Zou-Zou
                    and the lip-rounds of your breath
have fogged my rearview mirror
                    and what I can see behind
are the vanishing trees of a road
                    the darkness is gulping, and somewhere
I've been that I don't remember –
                    a bend that I missed in my mind.

It's the beat of the motor that brings back
                              the sexy way you yearned
at telegraph poles that leaned out of true,
                    your travesties of the Highway Code,
how limit meant whoopee to you,
                No Entry meant Lovely To See You!
how you told me *go sideways*
                    and stop inventing a road.

I shouldn't be writing you this –
                              I need to keep hands on the wheel –
But I'm harvesting thunders and bumps
                    like a doomed Ferrari ace
as the downpour begins
                    and my swift carousel bears onward
into the spill of the flume
                    and the windscreen projects me your face.

So please receive this letter
                    from a jet pilot *manqué*, a fixer

39

of broken-down trams, a cleaner
                    of graves, the mole who is scribbling you this
to the squeak of wipers, the drumbledum
                    of tyres, the hiss of the pissing-down rain –
a zithering flash for you my pale
                    ironic striptease, my flickering accomplice.

Night's coming down,
                    and my verse-lines vanish in darkness
and hard-to-see words go under
                    in serial dash-leaps at flight
and the road signs are pointing to battles
                    not to be found on the map
and the rusting litter of war
                    is caught in the beam of the headlight.

My flitzer has juddered to standstill.
                    God, how I've covered the ground.
A few cattle stand on high places
                    and the water is rising, sure but slow,
and I think of the deluge that's coming,
                    the malediction of the wet,
and the trail of that vermilion woosh we left –
                    our overflowing overthrow.

DONKEY JACKET

Reversed it's a bullfighter's cape.
It's the cloak of Sir Francis Drake,
made to be swung and dragged along the ground
for small feet to crush.

A coat
smelling of tarpaulins,
thrown across trucks
in rain . . .

Coming towards you, opening . . .
Outer Melton Fabric 65% wool 35% Viscose
A hand rummaging you . . .
Quality Nubuck Collar
The deep smell of wet wool . . .
2 Secure Button-down Front Patch Pockets.

This is the coat of the man
you saw on the down escalator,
his wrist stamped
with a blue number, like a pig.

Reinforced shoulders,
sailor-stitched arms and armhole seams,
a treatise on insurrection
in the pocket . . .

Breast fabric
soft as the navy.

YOUR LIFE AS AN AUTOMOBILE

It won't start.
You have it towed.
The rope grows longer and longer till the towing truck and
                              everyone else disappear round a corner.
You just stay where you are.
Remember how it looked when it was shiny and new?
Before a whole string of nervously jabbering girls
swung their ankles in and out of the passenger seat,
                              smoking and patting themselves,
and then a vast amount of suitcases, bags, trunks, coffers,
                              valises and miscellaneous debris
was loaded in and unloaded, leaving weight marks on the upholstery,
and scuff marks and smears and flecks of oil, paint, lipstick
                              and other substances,
and then a horribly prolonged series of moments that was actually
                              just a single moment
was followed by a juddering shock, and
people were saying 'O Christ!' though why exactly
                              it was hard to say
and people came running to see what happened?
They tell you: *England Welcomes Careful Drivers.*
You want to say: a) it doesn't   b) there aren't any.
Others drive by honking their horns viciously,
                              stabbing their forefingers at their temples.
A fat tear dribbles down your downy cheek
and plops onto the heads of the little African Babblers
who have gathered at your feet and are nibbling your old-fashioned
                              shoelaces with intrigued nudges –
such gregarious, fearless birds, you'd like to be like them.
The boot of your life is full of bullet-ridden corpses.
The aerial of your life has been snapped off.
There are bricks under your life.
A pair of unmoving feet are sticking out from under it.

A traffic warden arrives, with a charming smile;
she flips over her notebook page and your heart turns over;
it turns over again when she asks your name.
O and again with a sputter and lots of smoke when she writes it
    down.
Then she licks her pencil.
In no time at all you're in bed with a peaked black and yellow cap,
a black uniform with a yellow collar,
suave grey stockings and sensible shoes.
Everything's flashing; sirens are in whooping pursuit.
Close your eyes and hold on tight.

There's no other way to read this kind of stuff
as you speed across the dark horizon . . .

THE REVENANT

after Propertius

We do not die; as ghosts we survive.
> Last night the urn that held her heaped grey ashes
released a spectre. I woke in sweat
> to glimpse above the cold furnace of my bed
the burning gaze of Cynthia herself,
> back from the crematorium, same green eyes,
same dress, but charred, the ring I gave her
> eaten by fire, her lips cracked from searing heat.
A re-born spirit raged in her voice;
> she snapped a soot-encrusted thumb in my face:

'Think you'll ever sleep again? Traitor!
> Remember how you stood beneath my window?
Eagerly down the knotted sheet, I
> slid into your arms and we fucked like tigers
on the ground, waking the whole hostel,
> hollowing out the earth like my window-sill
with climbing out of it, mad for your
> embraces, doing that rope-act to reach you,
swinging there, stupid, on a ripcord.
> My sister nurses heard our every wild sob!

'The way that hearse reached the cemetery,
> you'd have thought it was a fire truck, me a blaze.
But *you* went no further than the gates.
> In the public viewing room, my casket stood open.
Someone tossed a condom into it,
> then triggered the switch that sent me to the flames
before the priest had droned his prayers.
> You didn't stand guard; don't bother to look shocked.
I know you've no black tie, shoes, suit – but
> wasn't I worth a bunch of discount roses?

44

'That bitch Clara, I'm prepared to bet
          put something in my food, tied my guts in knots.
Haven't you asked yourself what killed me?
          I'm twenty-eight; that's all I'll ever be.
I trust you reach crippled ninety-five.
          Betray Clara for my sake, right across town.
Petal is just waiting to be asked;
          Leila won't say no; Anne is anybody's.
But Clara had the whole football team,
          Sextus, in the shower. How's that make you feel?

'Fact is, lover, I bear you no grudge.
          When people read your poetry, verse is put back
where it belongs, in the world of tears.
          It's *my* name they'll think of when love goes astray.
Let cockroaches couple on this vase
          and hatch their children to grow fat off my ash
if I've ever said less than the truth.
          I was always yours. I never wavered once
although your friends were always trying
          to climb in my bed, do you a favour. Ha!

'Let Clara change the décor, Sextus,
          and paint me out of your life. Employ another
housekeeper, but give old Julia
          a pension till she dies. Please see her alright;
don't make her work for your monstrous friends.
          Stop writing verses; Clara couldn't care less.
Conquer your loathing of the graveyard
          and plant beneath the marble slab with my name
- on which I hope you'll write an epitaph –
          a dog-rose you've stolen from a city park.

'Or kick out that whore. Leave town for good.
      Abandon your thuggish friends. London's a prison.
The river still feeds the meadows where
      we built that crazy tower near our village.
Clear away the ivy tangled round
      the base and put these words above my ashes:
IN THIS RANK ORCHARD LIES CYNTHIA
ONLY SEXTUS KNOWS WHAT SHE WAS LIKE
Damsons droop their crimson clusters there
      and weigh down the boughs gently to touch your head.
Let the cursive of your pen find thought.
      Feel the life return that made you write for me.

'Ah, perhaps you won't. She'll not let go.
      But I'm there inside you, deeper than she knows.
Night has released me into your brain;
      the coming of dawn compels me to go back.
Clara can have you for now, but soon
      I'll reclaim you, Sextus – our dust will mingle.
Think you're dreaming? Don't you know my voice?
      How often have I whispered from the darkness?'
She spoke. And when she was done, I reached
      with both arms up for her. Straightway, she vanished.

THE OLD MEN BEHIND THE WATERFALL

Shadows murmur in the moist vault.
A brushwood fire ignites and flares,
throws a pyrotechnic script on the walls.
Trident-forked the flame leaps out and darts
and water tumbles down in luminous transparency.

Burn. Let water roar. And burn.
Ideas are millionthed in ash or simply
dashed by tower's deluge in boulder pools of clarity
where fish below the churning of the force
are bleak-green silverdull or swift and pendant and unsullied.

Prophetic age? Or time of stupefying?
Pouring or descanting, lifting or arousing,
in salivating fuses, spewing up the end of physic,
mayhem's sadness sweetens to a language-plunge
of firefall and waterburn, of river-blaze, of fiery deltas, elder-tongued.

ON THE MONEY

(Art's story)

When I was young, I coveted the money and the woman,
kept coaxing busy blood drops
from my reluctant thumb, grumbled out
the spell-cracked poems of a sorcerer's apprentice.

No rich. No fetch the ladies, either.
Then I saw an ad: 'Join *La Table Ronde*,' it said,
'accrue the benefits of debt.' I wrote for details. A pile
of bumf arrived, a plastic card.

'The upgrade, too,' I said. 'How much to be
a *verray parfit gentil knyght*, and what exactly is that, anyway?'
'You get to save,' they said, 'the whores in Avalon. We shall
assess you monthly for your acts of credit. Note, however,

that we like our fallen women fallen. You take the drift?'
The rumour of the ripple of a chuckle went around The Table Round.
'If reputation's what you want, we do provide a lake of it to swim in,
though any Lady you encounter there might very well be *wet*.'

More mirth. Sir Tristram-Sitting-Next-To-Me remarked:
'Decline the Lady's hand. The lake's polluted. It's a trap.
Do not accept the Windmill Chain, the Stretched-Horse Franchise.
Avoid the Hotel Camelot like syphilis.' Did I listen? No.

The Lady went to Hollywood to make explicit movies
for the hopeful. The vanes fell off the mills. The horses
wouldn't stretch. Someone torched the Hotel Camelot.
Men with clipboards came to query my accounts.

'I do not hear the rattle of your debt repayment, son,'
the judge observed. 'Twenty years of cabbage soup and chains
will hardly pay for your effrontery.' He smiled:
'But keep the memory bright of your lacustrine love.'

I moped for the duration. Released, I found a place to slump.
And then across my threshold rolled – imagine my surprise –
in an electric wheelchair, the Lady from the Lake, no less.
Her looks were gone and she was squeaky in a bonnet.

She handed me Excalibur (a replica). I stuck it on the wall.
The bills peck daily through the door – they give no quarter –
but I riposte with inky flourishes: a demon of the notepad.
We camp here on an edge beside a hole inside a pocket.

THE WAY

My first thought was: gone wrong again.
The smiling gent who sat astride his bicycle,
one suede foot propping him on grass,
was surely no policeman, nor a native of the place.
I didn't like his teeth. I didn't like his face.

That way! he exclaimed, and pointed.
I didn't like his ginger jacket. I loathed
his yellow trousers. What kind of riding habit
was that velvet waiscoat? And how did *he* know?
He had the smile of one who knows

you'll do as he suggests, and I'm the type
who knowingly will follow dubious advice.
I took direction from his finger. Not far
along the way I changed my mind, looked round
and saw no crossroads, nor the fellow on a bike.

The road was just an arrow into greyness.
Going backwards never is an option.
What to do where no choice is, but carry on?
Did I say that I was riding my Lambretta,
with saddle bags for all my gear, a jerry can?

Good I'd brought the latter, full of fuel.
There was nothing on the way. No filling
stations, roadside eateries, or welcoming motels –
dust there was, and flatness. Intermittent swells
of cloud and tentatively falling drizzle.

A ray of sunlight threw ahead of me
my shadow as I crouched on my machine.
I stopped for sandwiches, but they were dry,

as was my thermos flask, my mouth, my brain.
There was, however – just the one – a tree.

I made a mental note of it, a landmark, after all,
could be useful, though not the moulting bird
that occupied a leafless twig. The creature cawed
and, flailing upward on ungainly wings, let loose
a defecatory jet. Ahead was treeless waste.

I reached a river bank. My engine spluttered out.
The road stopped also, at the water's edge. No bridge.
I let the scooter topple over, took my leathers off,
threw down my goggles and my helmet, waded in.
Something in the water drifted. Something white.

It seemed to nudge my thigh. I caught
a glimpse of something glimpsing me, a look
as inexpressive as the stars, or leaves, or rocks.
I clambered to the other bank and dropped
to a reflective crouch. The river's drift

bore images of people I had known.
Each shimmering resolved a face –
Les, Ken, Jocelyn, Jackie, Bob –
I could name them all. Then the sun was gone.
I dried my sodden boots upon the grass.

It was warm – a damp alive humidity. Friends!
Could it be possible by power of the mind
they'd found a wavelength they could tune to mine?
Or was this just a chance-lit apparition? Come back to me,
I thought, be part again of what I'd wanted us to be!

A goat-path led my gaze toward the heights.
Up edge-attracted swerves, trying not to stare

into the precipice, I went in search of welcome:
women's voices, jugs of wine, a hallway, lights,
food smells, heaped-up bales of blood-warm straw.

But long before the summit, where the path ran out,
I saw the spiral of it, blank and windowless,
rising from the boulders it was built on. Built by whom,
I wondered. And for what? The dense rotunda of it
held neither door nor other means of access.

It made the darkest thing in nature I had ever seen.
I did a rather gawky jig, a pilgrim in a sweat-stained vest,
to show I didn't give a damn. I did not exist,
I knew, without a witness, and witness there was none.
The author of my being there was having fun.

And it was getting dark. I'd misjudged the hour.
What options had I? Wave a fist at it, let fling
appalling cries, or stand there pondering the thing,
which is as I've described it here? Turn right, then cross
the river. A twisting track will bring you to the tower.

THE POPE'S DREAMS

No more *grillades*
on terraces in late sunlight.
God hates barbecues.

No more toe-dabbling
in the blue waters of the evening.
God hates towels.

No more discourse
liberated by the white wine.
God hates bottles.

No more skin, no more
teeth, no more breath, no more perfume.
God hates apothecaries.

No more elephants
to ride on in the park.
God hates elephants.

More liturgical explosions
raising the neighbourhood.
More stale whiffs
from the body of goodbye.
More seizures in trembling cloakrooms,
to put it mildly

God loves you.

THE BLIND DOG

In the Hotel Egalitarian
the taps drip, here are containers
to catch the water, the bath tub
is big enough to hold a dog,
but the dog is blind
and bumps its nose against the taps
and the beds are too short.

In the Hotel Egalitarian
the grapes festoon the balconies
from which it is forbidden to make wine.
DON'T MAKE WINE FROM THE BALCONIES
it says in large letters.
The liquor is lethal, but if you chew the balustrades
they will release the sweetness mixed with bitterness
any pleasant view reveals.

In the Hotel Egalitarian
everyone wears yachting camisoles without socks.
At night when the power fails,
they pass each other with surly shouts and imperatives
that have to do with the end of free electricity,
shouting *Where's the dog?*
and other things
I really don't want to repeat.

The blind dog is trotting down corridors
no one has ever seen. It stops to pee at the open doors
of forgotten rooms that once held statesmen.
Meawhile the Hotel Egalitarian
organises moonlit trips upon the sea
for those who cannot read by starlight, and offers
hooks and line to anyone who wants them.
The squid are much too wise to bite.

On hot afternoons, round the hotel,
children play violent games
on bicycles with broken pedals.
The employees shoo them away.
If you are curious someone will translate
the gibberish the children speak.
It is full of mysteries and prophecies
echoing the wild grunts that drift
from the windows of the Hotel Egalitarian.

Bring your partner. We deter the easy visitor,
but the blind dog on the hotel steps will know
you when you come, and it will bark
its soft, muffled bark, like this.

PARADISE DONKEYS

Give me a country fair,
a half-cracked carousel, some tents,
a coconut shy, a modest crowd
in dust with country music.
Under the sun, I'll march away,
swishing nettle tops and calling out
to donkeys as I go: *John Hartley*
Williams is my name. I'm heading
off to Paradise. Why don't you
come too, my friends?

When we arrive, there'll be
a thousand ears behind me,
heads bowed and hooves together,
a donkey pilgrimage,
loaded up with watermelons,
or sagging under mattresses,
or in the splintered shafts
of rusting funfair caravans,
or yoked to someone's broken trap,
the whip still in its socket, quivering.
The Greek whose bray began in Troy
and echoed to Persepolis
will fix me with a patient look.
The angel waiting there
will lead us onward through
the season-heavy orchards
until we stop above a lake
and we'll look down and contemplate
our dumb arrival in a mirror –
silver ruffled by a breeze –
and see our looks of wonder slow-dissolve
to fathomless transparency

as we look deeper, glimpse
an ageless, white-haired donkey
nudging at his usual gate,
and slowly it swings open wide . . .

THE HOMEWARD HOUR

Beneath the stunned fragrance of the city,
a woman grips you as the train jerks.
Steady yourself against the priestess.
She exhales you on a furnace blast of air.
You climb lamentable steps
toward a drizzling, darkening sky.

The bus snags on soaking traffic.
It's pouring now, you have the seat no one can take.
Water runs down windows. A flood-pool
swept across the road becomes a wave,
an inundation. You glimpse a hand,
a clutch at something gone.

From the bus stop, you scurry home,
close the door and listen to the undergrowth.
You hang, nightlong, like a bat,
head down in the folds of a raincoat,
listening to parchment shadows rustling,
thinking of cellars and jeroboams.

Wait for the shutters to spring high,
for daylight, that clever detective, to find
your footprints in a flowerbed, reversed.
The steps that brought you here must now
be carefully retraced. Your journey is
a mystery. Rouse yourself to solve it.

The windows of your bus show those
of yesterday, their backs toward you –
faces you will never see again.
A cloudy orchestra is tuning up.
Beggars wail in doghorn doorways.
A blue declension grips your mind.

In a wind of dust along a platform
blackened flowers blow. Trains hurl grit
through mammoth workings; station names
articulate a liturgy. Feel the tide
of yesterday, how an arm reached out to you
and was crushed as the bus surged on . . .

MALCOLM LOWRY AT THE ZINC

The barman keeps you, brotherly, in view.
You're leaning at the café counter.
His gaze makes sure your shaking hand
still finds your trouser pocket.

Rum, *pinard,* whisky, beer for vitamins . . . ?
Aftershave if they've hidden the gin?
How about pulque, mescal, tequila –
another kind of drunk entirely?

Till you lay down in the street, Malc,
you were great company. The sight of you
could keep them happy five days long.
But sober on a forest path, you stopped.

A cougar stretched its length upon a branch,
and swung its tail slowly to and fro. To reach
the spring, you had to pass beneath
its gaze. Nothing for it but go forward.

Coming back, you stood beneath
the empty tree and saw your face reflected
in the slopping water in the canister.
They shot the creature, later, miles away.

On to the shack, the diving pier, a wife's
embrace. At night across the strait, a neon sign
blazed: HELL. A cold tide surged
along the inlet. The volcano stirred.

From deep in the inferno, an icy blaze
hurled upwards freezing ash that shed
into your paragraphs, echoing merganser cries,
sharp as stars or javelins of light.

Now a woman at the shore is waving.
You write an opening phrase, and look away.
It was a day like a Joe Venuti record.
The thunder-drawing peak flickers in the sky.

What do you offer, love, which drink does not?
The white November sun has brought
the dead back, living . . . *El día de los muertos* . . .
Paradise needs bootleg. A trembling glass awaits.

The barman, your accomplice, smiles,
although you haven't moved your hand.
Surprise me. Leave the money where
it should be. Stand the round.

PLOT

In the terrible garden of my old friend
the flies cast shadows, ghostly pigeons murmur,
a child undoes a gate and runs free.

The gate served no purpose. It was
a squeal on an un-oiled hinge. The child
has gone. Only the day lingers.

In the terrible garden of my old friend
the shingles of the house are shattered.
Sea-winds make the chimneys lean.

The hammock between the apple-trees
is not the one I used to read in.
A bucket holds dead water and wasps.

In the terrible garden of my old friend
is the high bedroom, where the painter
and Marie – she of the voluptuous warmth,

the shuddery chuckle – cried out.
The drawers of its cabinets are open.
Whatever was in them was rifled and taken.

Here it is that my old friend lounges –
a man who has welcomed ambition's departure:
the great pavilions, the secret paths, the talk . . .

Under cobwebs in that high room
a nude surrenders to grey light. From
the attic window, a cracked sky

discloses cloud and streaks of red
filled with people running, struggling
to hold horses rearing up at flames . . .

EARLY MORNING CATCH

Pale Jesus, dismount your bike
unzip your plum plus-fours
take a pee at the forest's edge
breathe the foggy air

Pale Jesus, catch a glimpse
of something moving in the trees
clucking redly up and down
do your britches up

Pale Jesus, striding forward,
place beneath your skinny arm
the escapee before it scarpers,
feel its heartbeat struggle

Pale Jesus, cycle home
mucho squawking in your basket
smile at its darting neck
remember where the knife is

Pale Jesus, cut its head off
bleed it gently, pluck it swiftly
cook together with its blood
in a pot of *Côtes du Rhône*

Pale Jesus, eat your supper
spoon the liquid in your gob
belch and feel rewarded, for today
you discovered *Coq au Vin*

GO

Go my opuscule
attract some deviant eye
open a door into the next room
blacken the paper with interesting marks

Go my opuscule
kick the proceedings off
speak with hilarity's sad voice
sing if you like, but out of tune

Go my opuscule
picture the reader's nook
the digestive biscuits, the bowl of tea
burp for your country, twice

Go my opuscule
edge closer to the one you love
speak sternly if you have to
make all your exceptions truth

Go

NOTES & ACKNOWLEDGEMENTS

Café des Artistes

Swastika: The meaning of this ancient sign is 'object connected to well-being', still propitious in Asia. The fan beneath which Mr Loneliness dances resembles what is known popularly as a sun-wheel.

The Drunken Boat

Rimbaud wrote this poem at the age of sixteen, by which time he was already well-versed in the uses of alcohol.

Ostrich Palisades

The ostrich, reputedly, will swallow anything. Popular mythology also has it that ostriches bury their heads in the sand at the first sign of danger. Both of these, if true, would have resulted in ostrich extinction.

Palisades (the military usage is invoked here) are strong pointed wooden stakes of which a number are fixed deeply in the ground in a close row as in defences.

His Life in String

Matthew Sweeney described a Canadian Indian storyteller to me, whose narratives were literally told in string.

Joseph-Ignace Guillotin did not invent the guillotine although he urged its use. He is said to have described it as: '*A little light refreshment at the neck*'.

The Reader

The book in question was *The Eyesight of Wasps*, poems of Osip Mandelshtam, translated by James Greene, and published by Angel Books.

The Garden of Ian Hamilton Finlay

Ian Hamilton Finlay described to me how an assault was made on his poet's garden. He had claimed his 'Temple of the

Muses' to be a religious building, exempt from tax therefore. Strathclyde Council did not agree and arrested three dryads. A subsequent assault on the property by the sheriff was wittily defended by the 'Vigilantes of Saint-Just', using 'the longest tin-can telephone line in the world'. Finlay's inscribed garden sets tank traps for the mind and fuses the natural world with the word and the world's symbols.

White Asparagus

Beelitzer Spargel is the characteristic white asparagus produced in Brandenburg in an area just south of Berlin. The sandy soil there is propitious for asparagus growing. West Berliners like me were unaware of the existence of this paradisal vegetable until The Wall came down.

The Revenant

This is not a translation. Elsewhere Propertius writes:
me iuvet in gremio doctae legissae puellae
auribus et puris scripta probasse mea.
(What joy to read to a learned girl
in her lap, testing my poems on her chaste ear.)
In my version, therefore, Cynthia's ghost commands him to keep writing.

Malcolm Lowry at the Zinc

Lowry's shack on the Burrard Inlet, in Dollarton, Vancouver, has acquired mythic status among Lowry fans. He built the diving pier himself. The episode with the cougar is recounted in his story 'The Forest Path to the Spring'. Joe Venuti was a jazz violinist of the twenties and the phrase quoted in italics opens a chapter in *Under the Volcano*. *El día de los muertos* is (literally) The Day of the Dead, All Soul's Day, occasion of an important fiesta in Mexico and *locus chronicus* of Lowry's great novel.